MW00945074

Spaces of Sanctuary

To Ursula
Enjoy the work
within!
Namaste
Maria

11-12-01

Spaces of Sanctuary

Discovering Peace &
Contentment through Prose & Poetry

Mario Starace, M.A.

Copyright © 2009 by Mario Starace, M.A.

Library of Congress Control Number: 2009904558
ISBN: Hardcover   978-1-4415-3532-0
               Softcover   978-1-4415-3531-3

All rights reserved. No part of this book may be reproduced or transmitted in any form or by any means, electronic or mechanical, including photocopying, recording, or by any information storage and retrieval system, without permission in writing from the copyright owner.

This book was printed in the United States of America.

Cover and interior photos by Annelise Rostig

To order additional copies of this book, contact:
Xlibris Corporation
1-888-795-4274
www.Xlibris.com
Orders@Xlibris.com
58042

CONTENTS

Nature
Introduction

Life
Introduction

Spirit
Introduction

DEDICATION

"This book is dedicated to Swami Muktananda, Gurumayi Chidvilasananda, and the great Siddha Yoga lineage for their grace, love, and benevolence."

FOREWORD

For millennia, words—whether written or oral—have been used to transmit information from one generation to the next. In a larger context, though, they have also been used to transmit information from Spirit to humans, from the unmanifest to the manifest. They have helped us remember our heritage, our ethics and our place in society, as well as our connection to the infinite.

The written word can be an astonishing tool. Used with respect and agility, it's the one medium that can have an incredibly incisive effect on our perspectives. We read for entertainment, while at times we read to learn. But when these approaches combine, they form a powerful catalyst that ignites our curiosity and passion to understand more.

No one knows enough about life. There are, however, plenty of sources to expand upon what we don't know, as well as what we *think* we know. The soul level poems in *Spaces of Sanctuary* will stretch the way you view everything, from yourself, your perceptions, the people and world around you, to the very universe you inhabit.

Life is a tumultuous journey that is often perceived, at least by most of us, to go by way too quickly. Transcending old notions and beliefs, particularly those that cause us pain and a feeling of separation, is a way to live with more faith, happiness and thus contentment.

Transcendental writing is a bridge from what we seem to know, to what we sense is the real truth. The words spring off the page and into our hearts with a knowing; we don't doubt them, simply because some aspect of our being *knows* they are true. It helps us to feel the awe of life, and the gratitude for all of its complicated-yet-beautiful details.

In the tradition of Henry David Thoreau and Ralph Waldo Emerson, the transcendental nature of the poems in *Spaces of Sanctuary* refocus the mind's eye onto a very different, more expansive and reassuring view of reality.

Poetry itself is a rarified form of writing, since it seeks to encapsulate one's experience into a tighter space than, say, an essay. And, in this compact space, the genre proves how the power of a few well-placed words can rearrange our neural circuitry forever.

There are collections of poetry that cause us to pause and think, and then there are collections of poetry that shift the very structure of our thinking. What you are about to enjoy will not only take you down, Robert Frost once wrote, the road less traveled, but also one that will make a tremendous difference in your experience of life itself.

John M. Calabrese
Huntington, New York
April, 2009

INTRODUCTION

My writing process began as a form of self healing in order to process emotions or deal with difficult life situations. Some of these situations arose within the context of the Mental Health work I performed for a living, and at other times was just part of the process of dealing with the problems of everyday existence. In creating spaces of sanctuary from these stressors I would take breaks regularly from my busy life and job to take walks in a park, or park the car near a woods or seashore and be inspired to write. Having once found a comfortable place it was simple to clear the mind of extraneous thoughts, allowing myself to flow into a semi-meditative state. That is when the understandings would arise from within, connecting me to places of wisdom and spirituality which amazed and comforted as I wrote them.

In allowing these reflections to arise, my awareness became heightened and a sense of direction to just the right words or images flowed through me from soul or Source. The initial swell of inspiration blossomed, and around it like building a beautiful garden, I placed the flowers and shrubs of sentences and phrases. Often the tricky part was knowing when the process was complete as the theme or title for each piece emerged as it was being written, and when I'd arrived in almost a circle to where it had begun a feeling of closure and completion emerged.

What's amazing was that despite writing at times about despondency, sadness or sorrow there was always a hopefulness anticipated in some form in many of the works within this collection. Spirituality of the many mystical traditions of both the East and West has influenced me throughout my life and is expressed in many ways within these reflections.

There is great gratitude inherent within this body of work for the ability to share profound insights, and a hope that not only will there be some experience of inspiration, but that some of the ecstatic feeling that flowed through me as I wrote will also be conveyed to the reader. If these writings not only entertain but enlighten in some way, they have fulfilled the circle of healing which can only come from the connection to Source which initiated them.

Namaste, Mario Starace

NATURE

Introduction

The natural world is such a beautiful gift, both simple and sublime in its majesty.

Many of these reflections were inspired by the mystery and beauty encompassed by nature in all her multivariate forms, not the least of which is the human body.

In taking the time to observe a leaf as well as the celestial sky, there is great grandeur to behold, as well as a call to uncover the depth of perfection inherent in these wonders.

Nature is to me a sanctuary which replenishes and nourishes connections to the core of the soul.

BEATITUDE OF THE SNOW

The breathtaking beauty of a blanket of newly fallen snow reconnects me with nature's comforting cloak.

Covering everything with pristine perfection like the perfect frosting on a cake, the white of winter's signature on the ground can mean bleakness or beauty depending on the view of the beholder.

With the blank page I determine what's to be written, drawn or colored creating shapes and forms with words or images.

In a similar way snow can be seen as a burden for weary travelers or as a playground of fun for joyful children.

Each snowflake is unique, yet all together forming a uniform pattern we can see as one.

What a marvel is the mystery of this moisture which under certain conditions becomes the frozen particles perceived only to melt again into water, and then rising up as vapor merging into clouds once more.

Maybe there is a message for me in this great mystery?

May I too make as beautiful a covering of my life, and in the silence of the snow discover the bliss of nature's bounty as beatitude for bearing what life brings and allowing this to merge with me.

BLESSING ALL THAT IS

Wondrous what nature does all around this world yet with eyes wide open we rarely see?

The trees appear to raise their trunks and branches straight up to the sky as if to worship and bless the life giving light of the sun.

The colors burst out of flower beds and shrubs enshrining surrounding earth with shades and hues no artist brush can match.

Lush carpets of weeds and grass fill the spaces with their traces of vibrant greens.

Blue green waters brush the shores contrasting the light which shimmers on waves like billions of diamonds.

Blessings everywhere, yet so often never noticed by the busy minds rushing here and there but not aware.

If such wonders are misperceived in outer realms, what greater gifts are forlorn within.

Forgotten too in the busy travails of everyday life are the instruments through which all is perceived.

Just like the trees, shrubs and sea, humans too can raise their hearts in appreciation when time is taken to commune with and bless all that is.

CELEBRATING NEW LIFE

Sitting outdoors in shirtsleeves says, it's really the spring again.

As the seasons renew life, so too renewal surfaces in a life to give new purpose.

Sometimes taking leave of old patterns presupposes the transitions that began under the permafrost soil of sadness and turmoil.

This makes the new sprouts of change even more precious to behold as the true colors of the new patterns emerge.

Allowing new beginnings their due process is something to be savored, like a fine old wine reaching a palate for the first time.

Favorable results are often experienced when surrendering fully to new shifts in awareness, like the lens of a camera focusing on a new object before snapping the perfect picture.

Perhaps the letting go of preconceived notions, beliefs and behaviors are the seeds for any new inner growth to occur.

Once the process breaks ground, immersion in the full experience of transition, connects directly to the celebration of a new life.

COMPREHENDING THE UNIVERSE

A spec in the sky many millions of light years ago is our sun to some far off viewer, maybe sensing others viewing their star in a similar way.

So what if the world we inhabit is not even a glinting pinpoint to the nearest solar system in this galaxy of stars of which there are billions.

The enormity of the universe's infinity frazzles the mind, yet is not the very essence of the elements that make up a human body the same stuff of stars?

Can it be that the consciousness which attempts to comprehend the magnitude of creation, is the same as that which exploded out as all there is?

Even now this awareness colludes to contain and sustain the universe, within this little thimble called the mind.

The great cosmic joke is, that once self awareness looks out into the infinite creation for answers to why and where from it all comes and goes, the echoes of the questions just keep on growing.

So now, how indeed is it to be comprehended?

Only by becoming again what is our essence, can we truly understand, as some scientist of inner exploration known as sages have said through time; turn within to sing again the One Song which is always playing.

FOLLOWING THE LIGHT

Glorious gifts given freely are those that when simply noticed, fill the heart with gratitude for life itself.

Watching weeds grow or clouds race across a clear blue sky, fills the empty spaces within mind's eye.

Through recognition of what is already present, the true blessings of the moment are perceived as they are.

Letting go of old patterns that no longer flow with living at ease with myself, is like allowing the scab to fall off a wound when new skin has formed.

No matter how much healing is wanted, it must run its course unimpeded by expectations of the quick fix.

Following the heartfelt tingle, to tell my story about searching for inner truth, is key to mental, emotional and spiritual salvation.

For I am truly the source of my own inner light, and the way to fulfillment of all that is possible within one human life.

Following this bright beacon is about allowing the light to flow onto this page Now . . .

FURTHER MUSINGS ON MORTALITY

A day in the life of a leaf is like eternity.

The Reaper comes in his appropriate season.

So why the great fear of our demise?

Everything passes but never leaves.

So too with death, life continues in another way.

Why derive such little comfort from this understanding?

Maybe knowing who it is, who experiences the change, over life after life is key!

Truly knowing that there is no end to existence, is crucial in comforting so called pain of loss.

When end finally approaches, freedom can come, in knowing nothing is really ever lost, when there is nothing to lose!

INFINITY IN AN INFANT

What would we say to the infant we were?

Holding the bubbling, gurgling baby beckons our consciousness to behold itself in its purest form, without judgments or preconceived notions.

Beautiful as children are in the innocent way of a harmless joy filled being, we could but smile and say, remain free of cares and stay in this happy state of wonder with the world!

Seasoned by suffering, the older so called wiser self would but shudder at this statement.

Nevertheless, that One whom we have always been whether infant or old man would transcend temporal trepidations; confirming again in one joyful sigh, the bliss which is every creature's birthright, to be in awe of all creation.

LIFE'S GREAT FOUNTAIN

Fountain old, how many birds have slacked their thirst at your overflowing gusher?

How dry and empty with winter's freeze approaching.

Leaves scatter around your once pond filled form, ornate in design, standing testimony to human ingenuity.

Cycles come and go repeating season's solstice old, comforting in reappearance, yet heralds of another time coming.

As the birds accept whatever nature brings, transfixed in survivals eddies and flows, we in our man made wonder, subvert yet are converted to be as they.

Ultimately are we not surrendering to our own nature's assertions?

MARVELING AT THE MYSTERY OF ME

Finally, I find myself at an age to know better than to dwell on misfortunes past, but not old enough to create more mischief in this life.

Whether wealth or poverty come, that semblance of serenity remains, which came before soul inhabited this mortal form and will continue once the vessel turns to dust once more.

So called morbidity can be a vision of true equanimity, but certainly it is not just in knowing mentally, but an experiential knowledge which makes this life truly exponential.

In finding myself forsaking the fickle second guessing of what could have been, I instead practice placing pure focus on that which is at once obvious yet elusive, the ever precious present.

In savoring this second as if it was my last, I come to know what living with full consciousness can bring; otherwise I'm but a beggar, forgetting what brings the next breath.

Instead of belittling the force which brings life, through the distracted meanderings of mind, isn't it much better to marvel at the mystery of me.

'MOVING STILLNESS'

Sky moves or does it?

Clouds racing across the blue expanse create feelings of motion.

Yet isn't all that we are hurtling through outer and inner space constantly, molecules as well as planetary galaxies.

Is it but the illusion of movement, or is the racing universe taking us ever into infinity?

STOP! Experience STILLNESS;
this is where all comes from and Ends; The Alpha and Omega.

It's as if we are in the eye of the storm evermore; at once connected to the spot within, from whence the Big Bang of creation emanated.

This is the space which is the Dramamine, for the motion sickness we call life.

Surely through practice some have halted illusory movement, and touched the space of blissful Stillness from whence we came and to which we return.

NATURE'S WAY

Feeling the falling leaves float down to merge with mother earth, is so freeing in the peace of their surrender.

If only humans could learn to let go as gracefully when their time comes, the brilliance ensuing from this would be so much greater than the autumnal colors.

Being able to follow the wind wherever it blows, but not letting go of the branch before the season comes full, is so simple yet profound a lesson to learn from the great master teacher of all.

Nature makes it alright again in her magnificent way, turning bright beautiful leaves to mulch, yet growing back out of this into flowers in the spring.

Maybe letting go is not giving in so much as allowing life to have its way, and in so doing becoming one again with its essence.

ON BECOMING THE REGENERATIVE PROCESS

When rain returns to refresh the earth it is a rebirth of a renewable resource.

Maybe it is all the many souls, floating in the ether pregnant with water vapor, waiting to condense again and flow into earth element, becoming vegetation and food for all creatures, eventually becoming the essence of bodily fluids mixing within male and female to reproduce and inhabit human form.

The sages say spirit floats on the *pranic breath flow, and when finally expiring out as the last gasp, merges again as wind air current returning to Source in cosmic respiration.

So too, many allusions of Creator breathing life into lumps of clay, which then become men containing in essence all that is; brings to mind the great panoply of nature.

For truly are we not the Pure inspiration of all creation, that can apprehend the process whereby we are, and in so doing always becoming more and more . . . . On into the infinite.

---

*pranic-or Prana refers to the vital life force essence of the body and the universe which moves through the breath.

ORDINARY SKY

Just another day of ordinary sky.

Yet why does it seem so special?

Seeing colors and clouds unnoticed at a glance.

But now I stare in appreciation at the atmospheric phenomenon above, and wonder why the ever changing kaleidoscope of beauty escaped my notice before!

PRAYER OF PRECIPATATION

Rain must fall into every life so that its moisture can refresh, renew and nourish the growth of new beginnings.

First tendencies are to take shelter from a storm, until the realization comes; that there is nowhere the troubling vicissitudes of life can not reach!

The difficulties that pour down drenching us with toils also make us stronger and wiser, as well as wet with the perspiration of perseverance.

So what is the worst that can happen?

The possibilities are that we can get wet behind the ears with experiences of life, take a bath financially, or face the discomfort of being left out in the cold, and feel the vulnerability of exposure to the elements of life.

These can be nothing more than passing moments of darkening shadows, on a cloudy overcast day.

Truly the great sun of inner Source is always shinning behind every dark storm cloud, waiting to illuminate our day once more, possibly with great rainbows, as the harbingers of blessings and good fortune the rain has brought

So like the farmer must we be, thankful for rainstorms, which bring new life for cultivating our inner soil.

Instead of being troubled by life's downpours, perhaps it is better to celebrate with great jubilation and gratitude, the gracious gifts that the heavens pour upon us from time to time.

SHIFTING INTO A RAINBOW

Ice cream cones and rainbows converge to confirm me in the beneficence of this life.

When everything appears to go wrong in not allowing for shifts in the gears of understanding, confounding me in gray storms of gloom; then is when a beautiful multi colored rainbow appears to clear and uplift my soul.

Even though atmospheric conditions must be perfect, to project the full spectrum of living light onto screen of sky, how many just go by, without a second glance? Not I!

Fully awestruck by this wonder of creation, I soar beyond my petty concerns into contemplation, on the mystery and beauty of it all.

So on arriving at my destination, I can appreciate once again the simple pleasures that life can bring, by simply licking the cold savory sensation of a sweet ice cream cone.

SIGNS OF THE INVISIBLE SOURCE

Thanks for the cool breeze, for the rustle in the trees.

Moving yet invisible the winds are always with us.

A blessing to sailors becalmed, moving ships of old at sea.

At other times a terrible terror indeed, tearing up structures and trees, with the furious fury of tornadoes and hurricanes.

Whether gentle or full of gusts, the same energy moves as that great force felt but not seen, except in its passing.

Similarly are we not filled with the same energetic essence, moving our breath whether shallow or deep?

A moving invisible force, keeping the rhythm of our respiration constant, for when it functions no longer, we are said to have passed!

So I say celebrate the movement as well as its passing; and so flow with the pulsation of energy, which is always emanating from the one invisible Source of us all.

SPARKLE OF THE SEA SPEAKS TO ME

Precious gems of light sparkle like shimmering golden tinsel on each individual wave of water, awakening me to creations collective kaleidoscope of living light.

One glistening glint of reflected sun ray, on the moving motion of ocean, appears to be there but for a fraction of a second, dancing on to the horizon.

But taken as a whole, the spectacle is but a glimmering illusion of sunlight reflected on the sea.

Are not we similar in our lives, reflecting the light of consciousness as an individual glint on the sea of infinity, yet suffusing these elements into their essence, expresses our own great divinity.

What that spectacle on the sea says to me, is that I am not illusory, but more that which is reflected from that bright array, is forever dancing with eternity as the essence of me.

SUNSET SPLENDOR

Sunsets are something special in that no two are exactly alike.

Scintillating rays of light in hues of pink, red and orange shimmering off horizon clouds, creating visions of grandeur no artist could ever match.

This occurs before our eyes every evening, but most are so busy as to hardly notice.

Why when nature makes such a magnificent spectacle to behold, do we often barely look up from mundane mostly mental concerns to see the splendor before us?

Possibly in recognition of the beauty of the heavens above and the good earth which caresses us to its bosom, our souls disinter in such moments of awareness.

At such times as the day's end, those petty thoughts which were held can fly to the sky which is filled with the brilliant colors of life's comings and goings.

So as the last glowing twilight hues fade to dark, so too may all the mental meanderings of so many lifetimes merge with the One eternal sunset, turning back once again into that infinite light.

THE ESSENCE OF LIGHT

The heat shimmer shivers up shapes on the far horizon that merge into the mirage manifested by the sun.

Light reflects back luminosity, letting all that fall within its bright aura glow in its glorious gleam.

Life exists because of the sun's rays which provide nourishment, warmth and welcome to what emanates from itself.

If indeed all life can only exist because of proximity to a star, isn't all that has been, is or will ever be the same stuff that is the essence of light?

So are we not the same as our Source, and the only darkness is that which obscures our connection to the light energy which sustains our bodies and souls.

THE MYSTERY OF WONDER

Smell of the Sea in my nostrils fills me with awe and wonder that such majesty exists.

Sky, Ocean, Stars all wonders and the greatest of all resides within my own being.

I am that universe become conscious, observing and attempting to understand itself.

This is the paradox of the eye attempting to see itself.

But what will reflect true nature of consciousness, except the peaceful pond of a quite mind.

Humans have observed nature, and seemingly conquered her elements with devices of technology, machines that fly and float and even travel out into the cosmos.

But what device can take us to the essence of our very nature?

That which reflects what is seen is the Seer.

So to turn back creation unto that primal wish to be, and in remembering, use that which we possess already, to know that mysterious essence from which we always are connected.

TREE OF LIFE

Sitting in the shadows of my family tree, I wonder how I came to be.

Thankful am I, for the many ancestors who struggled and toiled to reach free soil in their adopted land.

All so I could take birth and live as I choose, making my way as I say!

With this recognition comes the fruition of my lineage that I can return to root source some semblance of the sincerity of my soul.

Singing the song of who I truly am, is giving back to those yet to come, with a great and grateful heart.

So that one day someone else may say with wonder that is how I came to be.

For truly, are we all not sitting under our own wish fulfilling tree!

THE TREES ARE LIFE

So many varieties of trees, so unique even within the same families, whether Pine, Spruce or Maple.

Each standing tall and green, an individual, a work of art.

Branches and roots flowing out from their core, bringing light, moisture and life that can sustain even a mighty Oak hundreds of years.

Simply amazing to perceive, that from a tiny seed, such a huge living organism can appear.

So each life like a tree sprouts from nature's core to take its own special form; expressing itself in all its unique splendor, providing shelter and shade for others and sometimes giving luscious fruit to those who hunger.

If only humans could learn from these magnificent living forms, whose very wood becomes our homes and tools, to give back to life so abundantly.

Instead humans are indiscriminately defoliating hundreds of thousands of acres a day of plants and trees, to make room for cultivating and using the land.

In so doing we humans are choking ourselves with the smoke from the burnings, and cutting the oxygen available, that the forests provide for the planet.

If only human beings could see, the trees are life!

TWO AS ONE

Two trees growing like a V out of the same trunk say to me, that two souls can be tied inextricably, growing to flourish and thrive.

Two unique individuals standing side by side, sharing common ground, yet manifesting magnificently as themselves.

Tricky as it may be to distinguish one tree from the other, they are the same yet separate, as their branches and leaves spread out in different directions.

These two beings share the same sun, the same earth and common roots nourish them both, one leaning on the other when winds of change blow strong, gathering strength and support one from the other.

Bless them both for their union, but behold their individual beauty, which compliments and contrasts the form which enmeshes them in creations great dance.

LIFE

Introduction

This collection is inspired by the many aspects and facets of experience that life can evoke.

Since life as we know it is a temporary passage through eternity, a place of sanctuary along the way is essential to embracing and appreciating the astonishing enormity of this great reality.

It has been said that the unexamined life is not worth living, and so without being fully present to honor each moment, all the little miracles of life go unappreciated.

These reflections are both my examination of, and gratitude for, this amazing experience we all share called life.

A SALARY OF SERENITY

My soul is suffused in serenity, which spills over with sage wisdom through spoken word and written verse.

Specializing in spiritual understanding is the definition for what I do best.

Often enough, this does not equate with earning a living.

But in making life really worth it; there is no match!

So what is the salary for being inspirational, any perks or bonuses for great enthusiasm and euphoric ecstasies?

You may say the payoff is in the joyful experience, for this leaves a happy glow of self satisfaction, which is not purely selfish, but offers it warm heartedness to all who would step into its radiance.

ALL THAT WILL EVER BE

All things pass but their essence remains.

So many lives have come and gone from this planet yet their lineage lives on through the love they leave to those around them.

Whatever a human being creates with passion, whether a work of art, great thoughts, music or new life; that lives on as their echo into infinity.

For it is not so much the creation, but the essence of that, which makes an indelible imprint on eternity.

Coming into the great mix which is this life as we know it, so many tangible things take on such great importance in our thoughts.

Yet it is really the intangible soul, from which this all arises, which in truth is the only thing of any import.

So relax into knowing that when all that is now becomes dust, that from which it came continues, and always will!

That essence is the all that is and will ever be of us, at this moment and always.

APPRECIATING GRATITUDE

Appreciation for my life appears in a flash, as I ruminate on regrets and self recriminations.

Gratitude for the great gift of a glad heart, dispels the doom and gloom feelings greeting my mind a moment ago.

Memories of the love engendered for the departed remains ever present, making mourning for them a mockery.

Indeed to be downcast when I am so abundantly blessed by those whom I cherish in the present is paradoxically ridiculous.

Amazing how even a small shift to gratitude, can create a space for a flood of appreciation to abundantly pour in, where despair once held sway.

AWARENESS OF SPACES SURROUNDING LIFE

Keeping clear channels open, in the spaces surrounding my life, is the key to experiencing the clarity of awareness, as to how the inner space relates to the outer.

Perceiving with pristine perspective, how everyone and everything relates to me, is the cornerstone for living a life of revelation.

In keeping faith with a higher self-awareness, my self limiting tendencies are sublimated, for the wonderful freedom of living in harmony with wholeness.

Letting go of petty concerns, is about trusting that all is occurring for my highest good.

Without the constant companion of worry, I can once again notice the connective union with my deepest self, and hence with all surrounding.

When thoughts are allowed a looser reign, through creating greater spaces between them, the experience of blissful infancy can once again be had, only now with self awareness.

For in noticing the inner spaces, everything falls into place.

CELEBRATING THE WHOLE STORY

How we mark our milestones marks us, with the significance we attach to them.

Anniversaries, birthdays and such are just remembrances of beginnings, then why do we not celebrate endings such as days of death or divorce? Are not endings completions and should they not be honored more?

As a culture, we worship our youth and so focus more on possibilities in becoming, rather than the completion of sage wisdom, which sometimes comes with aging.

Bringing a balanced perspective can be a priority, only after conscious contemplation of life's circumstances, and how they play out in each drama created by destiny.

These are then sustained by our identification with the one who experiences the story, instead of the one who is writing the whole thing.

Leaving limitations hold, is allowing us into the awareness of the larger epic, in which celebration of the whole, is much more enjoyable then lamentation of the parts!

CONTAGIOUS JOY OF LIFE: (for Paulette)

Amazing how one life can affect so many, creating ripples on the pond of life, which keeps reverberating on into eternity?

Fulfilling the call to serve others is often the key in keeping faith with life's ultimate purpose, which is at once self-perpetuating and entertaining in the highest measure.

For in losing the self-consciousness of ego, the gains in expanding conscious connections to every other living being are immense.

Often those who have experienced a fall from social, physical or material graces know full well that Grace of the highest Source brought them down, so that uplifment to a higher calling could occur.

When this call is answered with open-hearted service, floodgates of joy so fill their lives that this spills over into so many others, creating a riptide of happiness, pulling even unwilling participants along in their wake.

What a blessing to have known one of these souls, who sang their song so well, that others could not help but join in their merriment.

For in allowing ourselves to be effected by such great ones, we too can become contagious, and share in the glorious gift of joy that is this life.

DESTINY'S DESTINATION

Delight in discovering the way life unfolds its mystery and majesty, making what was once seen as ordinary, appear extraordinary, and instead of what were difficulties, now opportunities for growth.

In all the random mayhem that can occur, there is a great concurrence of coincidence which when seen from a correct perspective, reveals the great patterned beautiful living mosaic of existence.

Sometimes things seem to occur too quickly to keep up, and at other times they appear to move as if in slow motion, yet all is perfect as it is.

Simply allowing what is already in motion to continue, is the great secret to being in sync with the cosmic ball, which invites us to dance in step with all.

To be in unison with creation, is that which calls from the deepest recesses of cellular experience, flashing forth as consciousness itself beckoning.

Whether one believes in the realm of spiritual dimension, or in a great nothingness, matters not, for destiny takes all to their destination which is perfection.

EMBRACING THE UNEXPECTED

Dashed expectations, expose the corners of desires for what they are.

Without welcoming change, one is doomed to experience reality in dreary doses of self created drivel.

To truly flow with what each moment brings, a modicum of gratitude for the unexpected must be cultivated; marking each experience as it arrives with an embrace, whether mediocre or milestone.

Maybe just knowing all that occurs is beckoning some deeper understanding, nudging consciousness towards Source in the seamless sense of wonder, required to open up the mystery of the mundane.

So, when plans go awry and everything appears contrary to expected outcome, rejoice at the opportunity to shift perception, and let go of the desire to have things turn out a certain way.

For in renouncing attachments to desired results, true freedom is found.

THE EVE OF NEW BEGINNINGS

In the twilight of transitions, sitting on the cusp of new creations, on the eve of a renewed life, I am celebrating a new year, filled with prosperous gifts of understanding and abundant vitality for new beginnings.

Being between what has come and what will be in the ever-present moment of creation, it's up to me to make it so.

I accept all the great blessings of breath, of bread, and of breakthroughs in perspective that come from the grace of destiny, and the great ones who have come before me.

Would that I be worthy of such gifts, for not in only receiving but in giving back is true prosperity earned.

Let the light of a humble heart, fill those who would search for compassion; may mercy and the bounty of contentment guide all who search for true happiness.

This ultimately leads back to heart Source, where the true treasure inherent lies gestating, just waiting for birth.

FINDING CERTITUDE

What way to turn in trying times?

Will the past prepare us with what is needed to endure and triumph?

Is the future beckoning brightly, or are terrible today's trumpeting more trouble for tomorrow?

So many questions, but from where are answers ever to come?

So long as the view turns outward, looking outside ourselves, we are filled with what we lack; it is only when we turn within, that we are filled with what we have!

Inner vision contains the clarity of contentment, when feelings of fulfillment reign.

Then whatever action is taken, the certitude of inner conviction and intuition, make the right choices obvious.

FINDING FREEDOM WITHIN THE FOG

Facing the fog, which can envelop a life, is the first step in becoming free of its obscuring power.

As the inner pilot directs and keeps a steady course in low visibility, when outcomes and paths are unclear, full faith and trust must be placed on the inner instrument, which is both compass and guide.

Otherwise, the vertigo of compromised vision, can lead to a crash!

Proceeding with caution in times of uncertainty is common, but following the inner heart's consent takes one quickly and safely to the most marvelous destination, arriving at certain CONTENTMENT.

Wherever one's heart-felt duty leads, is the only course correction needed.

It is not so much to be favored by fate, as to strive to fulfill one's destiny, which frees the human spirit to soar unencumbered above the fogs which life can bring.

FREEDOM FROM THE PAST

Fleeting are the freedoms that fall from ancestors past.

Holding fast to the past is mistaking the wake of a passing ship for the boat itself.

Yet even though indelible trails are left by those who have traveled this way before, it is up to the present traveler to set the course.

Nostalgia for what was, can become noxious when fawned upon, and acts as an impediment to fresh vision.

Is not innovation seeded in a new perspective, striking out in ways unencumbered with the baggage of prescribed formulas?

In so-called thinking outside the box, the inspiration to create, must be heeded and feed with the flames of courage to do so.

For in any time and place, freedom must be earned in the present, by those who are willing to act on a vision of what can be, unencumbered by the laurels of the past.

FRIGHTENING FEAR

On all Hallows eve, we masquerade as our fears, hoping to scare them away.

Ultimately facing the significance of this day, which celebrates the souls who have passed away, reminding us of our own eventual demise from mortal existence, is truly what is frightful!

But what in us recoils in horror at the natural course of life's ending, except the clinging attached controller called ego, which trembles at the thought of transition, from self created boundaries.

The initial terror of letting spirit be unencumbered, by the illusory hold of our mind made world, is the toll fee, which must be paid to have inner freedom.

So on the night when fear is enshrined and the horrible celebrated, it is fitting to remember why fear must be fully felt.

For when ego shrieks away from true Self in terror, blinded by brilliance brighter than a million suns, then self limiting fear based darkness, is frightened forever from our hearts!

GRATITUDE'S GIFT OF GIVING

Giving is the gracious expression of a grateful heart.

In order to fully provide a gift to some soul, our own well must be filled with enough gratitude for life.

When this appreciation peaks, it can spill over in its abundance to soak those near and afar with bountiful blessings.

Sometimes even the simplest gesture, such as smiling to a stranger, can light up a day for someone.

More importantly, the reservoir of good will within our hearts expands with each expression of giving, which allows us to experience our own great good fortune.

For in sincerely serving another with no thought of return, we receive the gift of our own good graces, and get to express thankfulness for having life.

In the great scheme of things, there must be balance, so when the wish to serve another creature arises within us, the pendulum swings away from simply surviving and fulfilling our needs, to returning life's favor for what has been received.

The gift which giving brings, blesses the one offering much more than the one who receives!

HOPEFUL PROMISE

On the edge of a new day, just before the flicker of first light, hope burns brightest within my heart.

Who's to say that any next moment is promised, except for the present hopefulness which exudes from my chest?

In truth are we not players on this stage of life at our own behest, or that of the great playwright of all.

This being so, isn't it better to throw ourselves into our roles whole heartedly, holding nothing back;
So that in the full light of day we can say, that the great song which was waiting to be sung for so long, finally has a voice!

THE ILLUSION OF SUFFERING

Karma rages on, as all unfinished business races toward completion.

The comfort is in knowing, that what must occur is happening just as it's supposed to, without our need to invest any more drama or angst, thereby creating more of the same.

Similarly suffering from any occurrence becomes needless, when it is understood in the context of the perfect creating more perfection.

Now this is all too cerebral, when getting hit in the head with a two by four! But after the physical pain and response to it has transpired, why keep dredging up the hurt from the blow?

Instead let it go, with gratitude that the head is still attached.

The great magician of *Maya* is at work, at once creating the cosmic trick of having us believe this is all very real. But for those who are aware enough to see her slight of hand, realization comes that it is all a great show, not meant for consternation, but for our own entertainment.

---

*Karma-refers to cause and effect of one's accumulated past actions.
*Maya-refers to veil or illusion, forgetfulness of oneness with true Self.

THE KEYS TO CREATIVITY

Merging with my own manifestation, makes maintaining balance, a breathtaking achievement.

Keeping creativity clear of fear, is the result of constant redirection of reductive reflections.

Whenever contraction appears, there is constriction of feeling thoughts, smothering inner being's ability to flow consciously into the awareness of creations many blessings.

Redirecting tension, which comes with uncertainty, is the inner labor that allows creative flow to occur.

Simply getting out of my own way, is what some so called gifted individuals refer to, when asked how their inspired work came to them.

It is of primary importance to first relax, when holding an inner space for any endeavor, in order to fully receive what is trying to emerge from the deepest recesses of awareness.

Once in creation's flow, maintaining equilibrium of body, mind and spirit is the key in allowing this experience to reach full fruition.

A LIFE WELL SPENT

Favorable fortune is often foretold, in a life filled with serving others.

From outer appearances this seems like a stretch, in terms of material outcome.

Selfless service doesn't always equate a large bank account, but instead storage of a different wealth occurs.

Whenever other's needs are placed over our own, a space of egoless simplicity, magnifies the Love that is latent within the heart.

In turn this joyfulness spills over into so many facets of life, and returns many fold, to bless us in times of need.

In sincerity, those who adopt giving as part of their nature, recognize that it is they who receive much more from their service.

Prosperity of spirit is fully abundant, in so many intangible but most important aspects of life, giving the wisdom, courage and contentment that money could never buy.

Beautiful and bountiful are the gifts that spring from a giving heart, and a life dedicated to serving those in need is indeed well spent.

LIGHTEN UP ALONG THE WAY

Sometimes vision is obscured by dense and clingy layers of attachments, making what is obvious unclear.

Like a path in the woods, made more visible in the winter when foliage is no longer clinging to every tree and bush; love is the power that clarifies fields of view, allowing the roads life takes to be cleared of the underbrush of desire.

Destiny brings many twists and turns to a life's path, but only the clarity of connecting to that power which brings the bliss of certainty, can keep one on course, instead of seeing dead ends at karmic bends in the journey.

Keeping faith with the core of every soul who has completed this trip, is the compass which always points true.

Letting go of extra baggage allows an easier passage, as the way can be narrow and tedious at times.

Being lighter and quicker in frequency of vibration, makes uplifment more perceptible in moments of duress.

Shedding the shadows of attachments, allows one to see more clearly where the light leads.

But never be surprised to perceive, that this brilliance has always been shinning from within, which is where it was conceived.

LIVING IN FLUIDITY

Finding some semblance of sanity, in the serendipities life can bring, is often the key to living in fluidity.

Just when obstacles seem insurmountable, and one more task is too much, is when finding the flexibility to pause on purpose to perceive a moment's pleasure in reverie, is of the utmost urgency.

Fleeting thoughts and feelings are not just procrastination at such times, but serve as the safety valve on the apparent pressure cooker life, which has been created or imposed.

In allowing a break in the routine, patterns are seen, which may no longer serve our greatest good.

A brief relief in the moment, can become a new perspective and lead to much needed change.

When rigidity is replaced by flexibility, the effort put forth is reduced, and instead of breaking down from energetic exertions, replenishment and recharge is what naturally occurs.

The certainty of change, encourages fluidity of choices, and then just like water we can flow with what comes.

LIVING ON PURPOSE

Why curse the fates, when we create our own destiny with every thought?

The great teachers say, that as a man thinks so he becomes.

To start, allow only thoughts of well-being to exist within the screen of inner consciousness.

From the sturdy base of only thinking well of self, success is measured by the inner bench mark of self-created fulfillment.

This attainment must be envisioned within mind's eye first, and then the experience, if allowed, will follow energetically.

The primary vocation of all is to be true to self first, and then allow the satisfaction of being on this purpose to spread in ever widening circles, so that this joy can envelop all aspects of life.

In the clear mindful focus, of getting the point of whom and what we are about, there is a ripple effect which spreads to so many others, eventually rebounding back to us, giving our lives the purpose and direction craved for, when before we cursed the fates.

NECESSITY OF SHIFTING MIND

Refreshing mental posture from time to time, is a necessity not a luxury.

Just as muscles and tendons will cramp and atrophy when not moved regularly, so too with world view.

A mind makes terrible trouble with itself, when stuck in the same place for too long.

Restlessness and agitation rear their heads, creating discord and discomfort from mental malaise.

Merely shifting perspective and stretching mental muscles, makes relaxation a reality once more.

Resting mind made muck with a little meditation, makes inner eye clear to see life in wider more wonderful ways.

Like a good stretch upon waking from a long slumber, a mind unencumbered by its own sense of self importance, settles into feeling a renewed perception,that all is well within.

Instead of the determination to dig ruts of mind-set, burying ourselves deeper into reflexive responses, simply relaxing into more open awareness regularly, is the salvation from dying mentally, before our time.

OLD HOUSE OF MY LIFE

Memories are made real again, by dredging up all the old stuff, sitting for years untouched in dusty corners of an old house that used to be my life

Mourning my dead past, as well as those whom I loved and are not here now, to get me through this closing chapter in my story.

Tears well up and overflow, carrying with them the final farewells for old things, and a place that reminds me of childhood passing into adolescence.

Having left that old house long ago, I never thought of turning back fondly to savor some semblance of happy feelings, remembering those called father and brother never to be with me again.

So I save what can be salvaged from that place and time, to pass along to another generation, hoping for my place in posterity.

Yet knowing full well that it all turns to dust, and only the love that we feel, remains in the hearts of those left behind.

ON LIVING

What is it to live in full attunement to whatever life brings?

Often the avoidance of pain, is suffused with visions of only suffering.

At other times, pursuing pleasure seems like a desperate attempt to prolong a moment in paradise.

Always the dread of death plays as a backdrop, for the clinging friend fear has become.

The flavors of living are filled with these feelings and more, but to truly taste the nectar of knowing fully what it is to live, one must be empty to them all.

For in letting go what is expected, that which is can be experienced.

It is in the space of stillness, that the essence of living occurs now and always, bring what may.

ON PAUSING

Waiting and watching, are the worst understood words. They imply patience, passivity and non-action, which in this fast frantic technological world means being left out of the fray to most.

Finding lasting value in life, may mean taking a deeper look at the implication of pausing, to witness what is unfolding.

For in taking the time out to contemplate action, more conscious choices can be made, leading to more enlightened experiences.

Is not the foreground marked in any picture by the background, and are not notes of music punctuated, by the silences between them?

In a similar vein, watching and waiting for the appropriate moment to act, is being in tune with the symphony of our lives.

The pause of peace, can precede any activity so long as the watcher waits with awareness, for the most fulfilling moment to move.

ON RETURNING

On returning from a journey, the comfort of familiar home surroundings seem at once strange and novel, yet inviting.

Amazing how human mind can find the familiar unique, but tires of the exotic.

Contrast is crucial, for spirit to find its epicenter.

Light cannot be appreciated except for the darkness; similarly dawn is celebrated each day as the return of light to the world, only because of the night.

So many symbols show this paradox well, such as *Yin and Yang*, but at the center of these contrasts remains, the seminal search for balance.

Becoming established in the inner realm, where awareness of opposites no longer has any effect, is where true center lies.

All journeys have their beginning and end in the Source space within, where contrasts, contraction and expansion no longer hold sway.

This inner core is where all life returns, has always existed, and is simply now forever more.

---

*Yin and Yang-refers to the symbol of a circle bisected into white and black, with a dot of black within white field and dot of white within black.

ONLY NOWING

Ending is just another way of beginning, cleaning out old files is freeing, and causes me to ponder how fleeting time spent in any one place is.

In clearing me of old ties to one type of service, room is created to expand into new opportunities.

Certainly one must leave a room, to enter a new place, so wherever I find myself, is a new space upon which to leave lasting impressions.

May I be glad as I go, to leave those whose lives have intersected with mine, a little better for the experience.

So never regret any of it, but strive to fill the greatest room in the world, which is that of improvement!

For in striving to be fully present wherever I find myself, there is no beginning or ending, but only nowing.

THE PEACE OF CHANGE

Transition times are often noticed, after changes have already occurred.

Looking for subtle hints which are the harbingers of shifts, allows for a smoother flow, with what is already occurring.

It can be a barely perceptible feeling of discomfort, from what was once certainty, or listening carefully and hearing something different in another's voice, or in one's own heart.

The times between, are truly great opportunities for recognition of the newness of each moment.

Aren't there times in the day, within the bustle of activity, when a pause creates such contrast, that new ideas or ways seem to appear out of no-thing or no-where in particular?

That space between, is the Source which is ever still, but from which all change and activity emanate!

Moments of merging, with this all-pervasive force, occur every second with our own breath.

For a millisecond between breathes, we rest in the space of our Source, but often remember not!

What a difference, to but notice the slight changes of transition, in so doing redirect the flow of awareness, to that supreme peace within ourselves and all around us.

PERTURBED BUT GRATEFUL

Just when I thought it was safe to feel happy, old concerns overflow into my life, like refuse coming out of its container.

More concoctions that ego throws, to trick my mind and emotions into believing, I'm the limited, contracted creature bound by these circumstances.

Once I have allowed myself to feel the sadness, which is the flip-side, and corralled these concerns; recognition comes, that I'm their creator and sustainer.

Similarly can I not call upon that great destroyer, who seems to devour happiness and serenity, to also consume the sadness, which comes from identification and attachment to these old reflexive feelings.

Ultimately I must be thankful to Grace in its benevolence, for revealing these hidden predators of my peace, and for creating opportunities for uprooting them.

May I have the fortitude, to sustain the attitude which gratitude brings, to all that comes my way!

THE POWERFUL PAUSE OF PREPARATION

A pause prepares one for the next phase of actions that must occur, for a completion to take place.

In the moment of rest there must be a complete release, for a relaxed responsive flow to next appropriate movement.

The breath is the greatest teacher here, for without the moments of stillness between inhalation and exhalation, hyperventilation would be the result.

Similarly, in life, allowing a restful time before taking on a new endeavor, is often the difference between harmonious ease, or a frantic stressful response.

Bringing a peaceful pause to moments of tension, can certainly avoid unnecessary negative reactions, which can later cause further regrets.

Incorporating times of stillness in some part of daily activity, can not only enhance mindful awareness, but contributes to the overall sense of well-being that most of humanity strives for in frantic activity.

So whether in doubt or certainty about an action, always take a moment of pause to reflect, thereby allowing inspiration to concur or deflect one from the course.

QUESTIONS IN SEED FORM

Where does the wind originate, and where does it return?

How is it that our breath keeps moving through us without notice?

What is the cosmic glue which keeps everything moving in perfect synergy?

More questions seem to unfold than answers occur in this great mystery called life.

The greatest wonder is that so many take it all for granted, rarely if ever becoming aware of the great mysteries surrounding all.

Great and awesome are the forces in play, around us every day!

The greatest surprise is simplicity itself, in the recognition that within the core of all conscious beings is the seed of the whole creation.

So as the fruit falls from the tree, its seed returns to earth, becoming again what it came from.

We too fall into the material world, forgetting we were and still are part of the great cosmic tree of life, and when enough of eternity has passed, we grow once again into our originating Source.

Who's to say what, how or where this occurs, except the One who sowed the first cosmic seed, to which we are all connected.

REFLECTING ON MYSELF

Everything behind, around and before me, is but a reflection of myself.

What is there that is not made of the same stuff as me.

The same consciousness that wanted to be more than itself, is who I really am.

So in this remembrance, I am fully present once more.

I have enjoyed the game of hide and seek with myself long enough!

A pause in this play, to savor the only One who can be found, is called for now.

So be it, that I have thought myself lost, for so many eons.

In this lifetime, the urge to remerge with the all that I am, has been initiated!

Nothing on heaven or earth, can stand in the way of this ultimate reunion, with my own nature.

RESTING BETWEEN,
THE STATE OF STEADY WISDOM

To rest in the peace of being who I truly am, is the key to living well.

Why not just allow the day to come, and have the awareness to appreciate the gifts so freely bestowed?

Sensations of satiation, still my frenzied mind, as in the first waking moment between sleeping rest and awakening to a new day, before the care and worries pour in.

Perceiving the perpetual clam beneath the stormy activity, which is normally identified as living life, is resting in the stance of steady wisdom.

So much to be savored, in tasting each experience, with a sense of newfound wonder of the expressive child within.

There is gratitude for each new breath, whether it brings exaltation or desperation, that respiration brings me the experience of this existence.

Comforting is the knowledge, that merging back with each exhalation, is the universal respirator, Source of All.

Are we not resting between the Creator's wishing to be, the cosmic inhalation and that expiration, sometimes known as the *Pralaya*, or the great dissolution!!!!!!

---

*Pralaya-refers to in Hindu cosmology, night following day of Brahma, period of time of the cycle of existence where activity does not occur.

SATISFACTION OF SELF, TRUE CONTENTMENT

Satisfaction with self, is the one service that an individual can provide to them self that is of true worth.

For within inhabiting this experience, comes the freedom to be exactly and fully what one is, at the core.

To let go of the cares that come, not letting others opinions rule, seeing the one light reflecting back through all that may occur; this is indeed more than any creed, and can serve to guide and provide, the inner substance for this journey of life.

There is no one to convince, of any truth other than the many pale reflections of ourselves, which when deluded, can but create the chaos of a turbulent mind.

Saving grace is to but experience Source of self, where once was the other, and thereby be an ungrounded lightening rod, for the many frustrated feelings, thoughts and opinions which are not who or what we truly are!

To be free to live fully, is to be completely contented with what is our essence, and share its bountiful beauty with all.

SEEING THROUGH SADNESS

Feeling flaky in the doldrums dump, is favoring self pity for the sake of suffering, instead of allowing the converse.

Caring for a saddened soul, takes a lot of effort, on top of anger at self for feeling so bad.

Belittling my aching heart for want of a festive spirit, is letting expectations exert their tempestuous temperament upon me, and leaving little of the temperate tolerant disposition, which is my usual set point.

How easy it is at times, for self-deprecating and despondent feelings to take hold?

My soul cries out for the stillness of peace, which is the epitome for the happiness of carefree heart, which seems like a long ago thought.

Safety in the numbness of dead emotional states will not be had!

Survival of the serene spirit, hinges on allowing the pain in and letting it go from whence it came.

SHAPE SHIFTING LIFE

What occurrences, or coincidences, or choices shape a life?

Simply possessing a heartfelt passion for something or someone, can draw that thing or individual like a magnet, thereby creating new connections.

The course of a stream can be changed over time by a boulder or a log-jam, in a similar way the obstacles and challenges in the stream of life allow for new directions, creating flexibility and resilience.

At other times, surrendering to what comes allows a life to flow with the waves of destiny and remain intact, rising above circumstances, thus floating on the sea of changes to ride out the storms life brings.

Through all the trepidations, exhalations and celebrations, this process of drawing attention back to the watcher within, who is both witness and Source of all experience, is the sanctification of soul.

The alpha and the omega, start and finish, all beginnings and all endings, are as one in returning to this center place, from which all forms are created, and from which a true life can take shape.

In order to change direction, one must first and foremost have a primary passion to search for this truth, which is waiting within the wings of our soul for revelation.

SHELTER WITHIN THE STORM:
Eye of the Heart

Could it all be coincidence, or is consciousness in complete control?

The vagaries of existence, and seeming accidents of occurrence, appear as destiny's great joke, except that sometimes suffering takes place instead of laughter.

So what of this cause and effect, sometimes called karma; is it preordained, or can choices be had to change what comes?

Clearly the great conundrum of ages, is a mystery shrouded in religious belief, superstition and fabled tales, which cannot be understood only with simple human intellect.

Understanding of the great mysteries, can only come to one who has passed beyond mind made creations, and sees with the eye of the heart.

The great Ones who truly see in this way have said, " *Karma is only the source of suffering when not understood."

When perceived through the vision of compassion, all of destiny's turbulence, is but a passing storm to the still calm center from which it emanates.

The Sages have said through the ages, take heart dear ones for you are the cause and the effect, and contain the shelter within the storm.

---

*Karma-see page 60

SHIFTING BETWEEN CHANGES

Free floating between lives am I, one not over yet, and the other having not yet begun.

Uncertainty seems the dish of the day, tasting blander with each bite!

If only the spice of resolution were to be added, it would all be so much more palatable.

Perhaps resolving to be resolute, between the certain past experiences and not so clear coming change, is the key to be free, in the midst of a shift.

The space between the breath teaches, that a pause can incorporate the peace of stillness; so this hiatus between what was and is to come, is teaching me the serenity of seeing this too, as an opportunity to be free with who I truly am.

Ultimately, does not every transition act as preparation for the final one, which if preceded by the correct understanding, is no transition but liberation of the soul, to be fully present while breath still occurs!

SIMPLICITY PASSING THROUGH TO SERENITY

Another year passes, but what of it, being again entangled in so many entrenched memories makes my mind want to implode!

The maze of images imprinted on my being, makes them all fade into the haze of a hurried life.

Fresh perspectives appear as an oasis in the desert, of a superficial fast-paced existence.

The seat of my soul cries out for the serenity of simplicity!

Something more is not what is needed, quite the converse.

To reverse this course, one must stop running the treadmill of believing that making more and acquiring material things, is the source of happiness.

This mirage must be perceived as illusory, before simplicity can succeed in seeding the soul for tranquilities arrival.

So then dawns the new day of appreciation, for each precious passing moment.

Each breath brings renewal, in the relief of a new lease on life.

Nothing is promised, except the serenity of seeing the world with the newborn eyes of the fully present!

To the truly awakened One within, it is always simple to see the serenity in the passing moment.

SOARING HIGH DESPITE ORDINARY MIND

The busy rush and hustle of an ordinary life, often leaves little room for soaring high within inner sky.

Settling for sensible rationed recreation, takes away the moments of spontaneity, that is the cradle of creativity.

For in allowing space within a hectic pace, a mind can take pause to appreciate, the precious gifts that life bestows with every breath.

In those fragile fractions of moments, there is freedom to see, hear and experience life as it is, appearing through the haze of frantic physical and mental exertions.

As the calm eye emerges in the center of the storm, the vicissitudes of living acquire a new vision, that cannot be submerged completely again by the waves of troubled activities.

Then flight of a higher calling, can finally overtake the busy activity of a hectic day, uplifting heart and soul to soar in joyous pursuit of bliss, which is the birthright of our own nature; despite being cloaked in what the great ones describe, as the ravings and cravings of ordinary mind.

SURFING THE WAVES OF WORRY

When the waves of worry well up inside my at times scattered mind, the choice is mine to drown, be washed away or surf.

Certainly, riding through anxiety takes balance, some training and a sturdy board for support.

That vehicle for sailing above the many high waves of mental agitation, is my practice of meditation.

Marvelous how some little time spent each day, mending the ripples of care and woe in a weary mind, can weave such a beautiful state of equipoise when needed.

Staying steady as the sea of change churns up its endless ebb and tide, is key in keeping faith with the flawless still space of the inner Self.

This much deeper state appears more frequently, when conscious effort is put forth, to make contact with this dimension of myself.

As the serenity and certainty of inner peace expands, through this meditative practice, it spills over into everyday reality, causing centers of equanimity within the busy bustle of life.

So, when the waves of worry appear to engulf me, all I must remember is that, 'Surfs Up.'

SYMPHONY OF FLUIDITY

The fruition of fluidity, feels like the lightness of a feather, floating on a breeze, mixed with the force of rushing water.

Fleeting yet forceful, is the state of flowing with life's own energies.

Once allowed, the stream of energy comes through us, then everything appears effortless, there is no more resistance, since this flow of life has always been existent within.

Savoring this seamless reality, which co-occurs with what is believed to be ordinary awareness, makes each new moment an extraordinary event!

There is no place to be in space or time but here and now, which is the ever present throb of consciousness, pulsating within and around us always.

So amazing, that the great life force has taken so many shapes and forms, for its own amusement!

When this power reconfigures into its essence, solidity and fluidity no longer hold sway.

Instead, the realization comes, that this great mystery can unfold as a symphony, of which we are but the notes, and at the same time complete as the whole piece.

THE WAY OF FLUIDITY

Fleeting fluidity frees me, from contracting into believing I must always be in control.

The consequence of living this illusion most of the time, makes for a constipated uptight existence.

Transformation comes in glimpses of occasional freedom from the tyranny of this idiosyncratic ego's way.

Maybe instead of the fear of drowning in unknown waters, the ability to float freely is directly related to letting go of this false idea of always being in charge, and allowing the tides of life to take me where they will.

Since destiny's decrees come unannounced, why strain to hear what is coming, and thereby give power to the delusion of believing the echoes of what was will be now again.

When set adrift in this world of time and place, it is better to relax than to struggle, for in allowing to let go, the way of fluidity is found, freeing my whole being to flow perfectly with what comes.

THE VALUE OF SIMPLICITY:
SEEING ONE IN ALL

The appearance of everyday experience in modern life, is tainted with too much trouble!

Underneath the busy bustling surface of material existence, is the longing for simplicity and some stillness.

For when technology overwhelms its creator, with an inability to manage it all, its time to simplify.

In the never-ending quest to accumulate more stuff, the ability to appreciate anything is lost.

Better to care for a few possessions of quality, than to contribute to the corrupted culture of consumerism, which encourages the constant acquisition of disposable environmentally polluting junk.

So, what are really true needs of human beings, but to live in harmony and well-being with surroundings and community; where cherished time tested values contribute not to consumer profit, but to the common good and uplifment of the individual.

To truly pursue happiness in society, a return to simplicity is indicated, as well as the value of the one, must be supported by all.

TRANSCENDING THE I POSSESSIVE

Battered, benumbed and betrayed are we, by our own inner treachery.

This is fueled by the sense of self-importance, which is the great trickster leading to obsessive indulgence in the illusory, I possessive.

Putting a stop to the relentless neediness of self-aggrandizement, is but a simple switch away.

Pulling the emergency brake on ego's runaway train, is stilling mental chatter or self talk, with ancient disciplines as fresh today as ages ago.

This inner troublemaker is our own creation, which can be stopped by holding the mirror of consciousness up to our inner awareness.

Simply stilling the tendency to keep illusory worlds within whirling around, takes away their gravity, so that the puffed up person we think we are just floats away.

Indeed the true Self known by many names, is the one and only one, who can triumph over the treachery of the trickster within.

Finding the path, which includes the company of a liberated one, makes the way to this inner realization much easier.

For ultimately, in finding the true Self, we need help in first losing the false.

WRITING LIFE'S STORY

One chapter closes, leading almost seamlessly into a new story.

Well written some would say, but the writer must be satisfied with his own work.

What is it that makes one understand, that in truth we are all the authors of our own life story?

At any time, the tense can be changed from the narrow first person singular, to the more inclusive third person plural.

It's all in the writer's perspective; making the connections to view life in a more all inclusive manner, is but a slight shift in awareness.

In recognizing the unique perspective and creative gifts that are within each one's innate ability to shape a world-view, we can translate this vision, into something shared and cherished with others.

Isn't this something any great author would say in their own way; that the ultimate creator imbues creation with his own living essence, which when fully appreciated, take on its own life and continues the universal story which never ends.

SPIRIT

Introduction

The vital essence emanating through the core of who we are is said to be Spirit, the ultimate sanctuary.

This universal Spirit filters into our very being, igniting and sustaining the energetic power which is life itself, as the individual facets of a greater force.

Intangible yet ever present, this all pervasive consciousness is the guiding presence that, when heeded unfailingly, brings meaning, depth and substance to a life.

Mysterious in its ability to penetrate all realms of awareness, Spirit is responsible for all the great inspiration and creativity that flows from our souls.

The qualities of joy, contentment and inner satisfaction are but shadows of the radiance of a human Spirit fulfilling its purpose, to know itself completely.

AN ANTIDOTE TO ANXIETY

Weary of worry, of woes upon woes, yet still I return to this pattern like a whore who knows no other work. Following familiar tracks, even when it becomes obvious they lead to a dead end.

Dismay may become distended when not distracted by even a drop of detachment.

For in that moment of stepping back from the brink of despair is the prayer of deliverance from despondence.

Frequently I find that if the flames of anxiety are fanned high enough by fear, watching what rises from their ashes is answer enough to try some trust.

Feigning faith in the face of fears, brings others some relief, but does nothing for the one faking it!

Forgoing further friendships with fear is the only course that can be clear, as my essence acknowledges the truth that love and fear can never coexist.

Thankfulness tried and true is the companion of the fearless!

Given the grace of a thankful heart, trepidations are terminated, for the only true antidote to anxiety is the trust of a loving thankful soul.

AWAKENING THE DREAMER OF THE DREAM

When will I wake from this long dream called life, conjured up by consciousness?

Some say that only by dying can one be born to eternal life, but without truly waking, what's the use of just entering another part of sleep?

As with any conundrum, at first there seems no way out!

Am I Doomed to dream my life away as I gently row my boat to shore upon imaginary shore, never finding grounded awareness?

Finding the few who know the dreamer of the dream, is the clue to the great puzzle presented.

Perhaps through meeting one who lucidly creates the dreamscape upon which all dreams are based, can I catch on to the great game?

Like a contagious germ, this ability can flow from one awakened dreamer to another, creating the dawn of new awareness, which peaks through the sleepy veil even once and can never be forgotten.

Even now, as I write these words, I'm navigating closer to knowingly directing my dreams back to awakening.

Maybe an awakened one is now shaking me out of my slumber as I write this?

AWAKENING TO TRANQUILITY

Sleepwalking through life transfixed on petty concerns is the way of the masses.

Maybe melting into this gray flow of mundane mendacity, makes the misery of this more bearable; with so many sharing the same deluded reality?

Every once and awhile a few wake up, and are promptly set upon as if by disturbed zombies, hungry to tear apart anything different from the living dead illusion, they believe to be life.

Silence surpasses all concerns when awakening!

Simply allowing inner calm to have its day, and not setting off the clamor that can cause disturbance with those still asleep.

Truly much good can be done by one who is fully awakened, while the many are snoozing.

However, when enough good souls are fully awake to their own nature, a shift can and does occur, even for the somnambulant, creating the dawn of a new age.

Certainly some will sleep 'til noon, but eventually the light of a new day will have its way.

AWE AND WONDER OF IT ALL

Why let wonder go, when all that we are is a mystery even to ourselves.

There are so many astonishments that occur daily, that are taken in passing as the background of our everyday existence.

How does our breath keep us alive from moment to moment, even though we don't fully understand these phenomena, yet take it away for even a short time, and the body ceases to function?

Can anyone fully explain how even the tiniest forms of life came to be on this planet, yet we pass the miracle of spring season often without a second thought as to the perfection and balance of nature?

Awestruck by the very essence of existence are a few great ones who truly live, they tell us most of all, to appreciate ourselves as the Source of all that is.

BEING BLISS

Feeling good is more than tactile sensation.

It encompasses, true inner elation.

But from where does this experience arise?

I know it is more than the sum of emotions it does comprise.

Elusive ever-fleeting joy, wants to be coy.

But I intuit that there must be more to it.

So to recreate a happy state, appreciate!

And never forget, that being bliss is never a miss.

BENEVOLENCE OF THE BREATHLESS

Between light and darkness, joy and sorrow, abundance and scarcity, lies the key to conscious contentment.

Remaining steady, stalwart and serene through the victories, as well as the tragedies life brings, is a sign of the saintly sane.

Being in the still center between beginnings and endings, begets the benevolence of the breathless.

Those who notice the pause between the breaths can expand that stillness, to serve many courses in steady wisdom, to the ever ravenous mind.

Preparing not for the calamities that may never come, nor expecting the windfall profits from a pursuit of happiness, is peering into the ever present now, which has never been past and will never be tomorrow!

Being, is noticing with full awareness in this moment, taking consciousness beyond contrasts to the core of contentment, which is waiting like a sprout in the earth for the spring sun of serenity, to summon its green splendor once more.

THE BREATH OF PEACE

Controversy, conflict and contention boil over, from a frenzied stress driven life.

Forgetting to pause and breathe in the peace, which is the gift of being alive, brings in the belligerence of the breathless.

Becoming shallow starts with contracted respiration, brought on by the feeling of being at the effect of it all.

Simply surrendering a moment, to savor the taking in of the life flow, stops the constriction, connecting us once more with our Source.

Watching the gentle breeze blowing through the trees, can be just the reminder to take the moment in fully with our very own breath; allowing for that fraction of a second's stillness, to put all fit-full activities into proper perspective.

For without the next inhalation, where would we be but expired!

THE CLIMATE OF CONSCIOUSNESS

Translucent white light, shimmering like snowy ice, sets my soul to shivering.

Clouds shrieking across a clear windy sky, passing patches of condensed moisture ripe with rain, reeling past my vision like dark thoughts passing quickly within mindscape, scattering turbulence throughout my being, loosening tear ducks which release like raindrops falling down my face.

Feelings pass quickly, like the energy in motion they are, bringing the calm after the storm, so that the peace of a full release is welcome.

Within the safe harbor of serenity, the passing upheaval seems like a bad dream.

But who indeed is the dreamer, and why is emotional climate so variable as to be turbulent one day and serene the next?

Maybe there is not only one inner climate that is worth experiencing, but all have their effect on the weather of life.

Whether temperate one day, or stuck frozen in a cold state another, it is this variety that contributes to wholeness.

Every so often one can find that the creator of climate is the dreamer of life itself; which once set in motion must have its effect, yet not necessarily be at the effect, of the patterns thus created.

COMPASSIONATE INTERCESSIONS INTERSECTING

The intercession of saintly souls comes, when a single life intersects with compassion for all.

Faith is flawed, when blinded by dogma that doesn't see the suffering of supposed sinners.

Those holding judgmental court over others whose beliefs do not agree with their own one true construct, remain stuck in the idea of the self-selected saintly few who are saved!

Why believe grace is hidden behind only certain select doors, when in reality it blazes abundant as the sun, on all with eyes to see.

Then can not a heart but melt, when connected to that light which illuminates all, especially when confronted with the sea of suffering humanity, hungry for the warmth and comfort of the luminosity of Source.

One, who heeds compassion's call, stands for all who would willingly allow the gratitude for grace to shine through them more fully!

In being so willing to serve another, the angelic hosts make manifest their intercession, through the love exchanged from one to the other.

For in the loving intersections of so many lives, lies the brilliant light which shines through all, as compassion calls.

COMPASSION'S CALL

Considering compassion to be a conscious choice, is the first step in cultivating consideration for all living beings, most of all ourselves.

Keeping kindness near, as a dear companion on this journey of life, makes the path brighter, lighter and a more cheerful way.

The possibility of appearing vulnerable is the price of admission for feeling more fully, with an open heart.

Being more attuned to others plight and suffering, takes the gentle courage of one who has allowed themselves, to pass through their own portals of pain.

Only one who has passed through their own dark night of soul, can fully appreciate the resultant light of transformation, and can then encourage those who still may be in throes of their darkness.

In the end, love dispels all suffering, by simply allowing an unconditional inner perspective to seep into ever aspect of life, and deliver us and those around us to that higher frequency, which is compassion.

COSMIC CONTEMPLATION

Everything exudes its own energy, so glow with the flow and be the *Chi.

The pairs of opposites interact within the circle of light and dark, creating contrast but also colluding with each other, to form a whole experience.

Whether setting sun or rising moon, the celestial show goes on for many curtain calls, filling ears that can hear with the music of the spheres.

Another round please, is the universal call, as consciousness becomes filled with the intoxicating elixir of its own making.

Only the stillness of space can absorb the super nova of stars, spilling over and seeding new solar systems.

Similarly, only inner stillness allows the small self to disintegrate, thereby realizing absorption with Source energy once more.

One certainty exists, within the great panoply of creation; that only change is certain.

Within transmutation lies the key that unlocks the mystery, that within every molecule resides the refined space, from which all emanates and returns.

---

*Chi or qi-refers to the Chinese word which is an expression for the natural energy of the universe.

CROSSING DREAM ILLUSIONS

The passing dream of a life, but a blink in God's vision, yet all there is, ever was or will be, is contained within His view.

Storm tossed upon the shore of a world, we are washed out of a womb of forgetfulness, only clinging to still remembrances, of a once oneness with all.

Oh, Navigator of the vessel, take me through illusion's struggle, to origin's root center, tranquil once more.

CURRENTS OF CONCIOUSNESS

The waters of life flow by, sweeping whatever withholds itself or not into its currents, thus consummating the purpose for existence.

Individuals may manifest delusions, thinking they are unmoving, even as they are carried away by the current to the falls.

Yet those who recognize the current for what it is can navigate a course to quiet ponds or the safety of a stream.

Struggle against inexorable currents is certainly futile, but so is the thought that one is being swept to their doom.

The sanctity of sanity, lies in acknowledging being wet by the waters of life; knowing full well, that the choices made while being carried along by the current, like the trim of a rudder, steer us to life's destinations.

A way is created in choosing a course that may take us to some safe harbors for a time, but ultimately the journey will end as it began, with a merging into the sea of eternity.

Along the way, a sanctuary of space within can appear, which when entered, allows the emergence of knowledge that the water and we are one!

Once dissolved into our essence, the recognition comes, that the current is that consciousness which we always were.

DESPONDENCE TO DIVINITY

Descending into the depths of despondency is a denial of the existent ever-present pleasure of simply living in the presence of divinity.

Precisely when toxic emotions such as anger, and its self indulgent cousin depression appear on the mental screen, is when this undercurrent of feeling like a bubbling stew can overflow the mind pot, providing an opportunity for cleansing the impurities of misunderstandings and mistaken identifications.

With a full regurgitation of these poisons from the internal consciousness system, the soul can once again assimilate back, to original Divine Source.

The apocalypse of darkness within human experience, with its attendant horrors of cruelty and corruption, can not exist when the lamp of divinity is lit within enough of humanities collective soul.

Then that light will dispel the dark night of the soul, bringing the birthright of every being's connection to wholeness, back from the brink of despair.

Beware the trickster within mind, whose power lies in proud identification of me and mine; he is the one cause that keeps the darkness there.

When the light of pure existent consciousness shines through this false faker's façade, it is simple to see that the one brilliant seed of all, resides ready to reveal its true form within the human heart, which is the true divinity of pure I am, that I am!

DESTINY REVEALED

Appointments with destiny can not be broken, but attachment to the outcome can.

Bearing up under difficult circumstances, is more in how they are seen, than what they bring.

Whatever an individual holds dear to their heart, is key to responding to what life brings.

If the qualities of understanding, tolerance of opposites and compassion prevail, then whatever comes, the response is steeped in love.

When it becomes clear that whatever is called for in any situation is not what or who we are, but simply an appropriate response, then destiny can only bow before such a one.

From the highest perspective, everything and everyone are behaving exactly as they are supposed to.

So then why be affected by this dream, which destiny unfolds?

Instead, consciously strive to awaken from this ageless *Karmic* sleep, recognizing that it is all our own creation.

Karmic-refers to Karma, see page 60.

FALLING THROUGH TO FREEDOM

Timeless breezes blow through me, as if to take me here and there.

Back and forth, to emotions that have held sway for seeming eons.

How many countless lives spent, driven from one compulsion to another?

Always a slave of fear of pain, yet brought to this very anguished expectation.

No more this time! Staying steady, rooted in the Rock of present moment, I watch as emotional turbulence attempts to catch me up in its tornadic funnel, appearing to spin ever faster, creating the dizziness called ordinary life.

I choose to stop and watch, as if from a distant place, perched on the ledge of Inner freedom, I allow myself to surrender and fall through to infinite Stillness and Peace, that passes understanding.

FALSE SELF-CREATION,
OR THE WAY OF WORDS

Extolling non-existent virtues is truly an exercise in futility, for in trumpeting those qualities which appear as treasures, turns any semblance of sincerity to ruin.

Beneath the brilliant seeming surface of self-created delusions, lies the rot of pride.

The pact which an individual makes with themselves to perpetuate ego centered perception, is the path of the peripheral and shallow.

The sublime way of true soul, subsists in the singularity of silence!

Settling for the way of wonderful words, is like believing oneself awakened, while still asleep.

The joy of creation can be welcomed only by one, whose heart is not so full of false self creations.

FINDING SOURCE OF MIND

Fickle mind, fleeting from one thought to another, savoring none.

Swaying through emotional pitches like an energetic roller coaster, never staying steady but careening up and down with unpredictable turbulence.

Latching onto one desire after another, never allowing fulfillment to have but a brief moments reign in your mental kingdom.

A friend would say to such a one, to stop such crazed activity even for a few moments and so savor the power, which is the source and sustainer inherent for this frantic pace.

Just as a child absorbed in play pays no heed to another near, so too dear mind do you go on consumed in many illusory dreams, never noticing the One who watches and allows all this to be!

With a gentle loving steady voice, heart Source, can bring mental agitations manic dance to a slow fading halt.

Only then, when flowing from steady wisdom will the mind be the great magnificent creation intended, operating only when bidden by the One who set it to think.

FLOATING FEARLESS

At times fatigue flattens me, so that I want to just fall on my back and gaze at the blue cloudless sky until I feel like floating fearless, like a feather on the breeze.

Then breathless, do I reconfigure my conscious mind to re-create this tired feeling, back from whence it came.

Often I catch myself careening full force into the many turmoil's and travails of everyday existence, never allowing the precious pause of peace to take me back from the precipice of self-exhaustion.

Shaking off the many mental mantels I have worn can wear me out, but ultimately it is well worth it, as the less the weight of self importance carried, the more enlightened the feeling.

Consequently, the tired but true emotional states when overburdened, will either breakdown or create new pathways of experience; much like a muscle torn from resistance weight training will reconfigure into a harder but stronger leaner entity.

It is such a powerful paradox, that in order to be uplifted one must first fall exhausted by the weight of the world, only then can the letting go occur that must for floating fearlessly through life.

FLYING FEARLESS WITHIN INNER SKY

Soaring in celestial skies seems like an alibi, for not being fully grounded in so called material realities.

Floating above it all, as if gravity need not apply, is only for those who have lost their fear of falling.

For in tempting fate, with the fearless abandon of one lost in ecstatic experience, just one thought not congruent can lead to a crash!

So when in flights of euphoria, flee not from the mundane material world of the mortal.

Instead spread the wings of surrender to the sacred inner sky, and float on the thermal winds of the world whizzing by.

FROM THE PERFECT COMES THE PERFECT

What can prepare one for the experience of perfection?

One moment my mind is filled with the frantic activity of what was, could have been or will be and in the next, there is nothing but the clear crisp awareness of this very moment!

In the still serenity of the present perfect instant, there is nothing to achieve or conceive, but just the purity of being.

It is as if the world stopped, and now I can see how every detail and the seemingly contrasted imperfections fit perfectly into the scheme of things.

This is not so much a mental vision, but an experienced feeling of certainty that all is well with me and everything else.

The joy that converges upon me at these times is inexplicable, but I recognize this happiness as the undertone for everything experienced.

Yes, even in the depths of grief or madness, there is a bubbling bliss beneath the chaotic surface, from which all has emanated and all returns.

So if anything is taken away from the perfect, perfection still remains . . . .

ILLUSION OF MOVEMENT

The illusion of movement is apparent, because the one who watches is always still.

Just as the waves appear to move with the wind and current, the ocean is still the same.

So too in the hustle bustle of everyday life, many things appear to be happening, but inner witness remains ever watching from the still center at the Source of being.

If an object moves as we watch, often there is a sense that movement occurs to us, even though this is not so.

In the same way the universe is in constant motion, yet from where has it come and where is it going?

Infinity is never defined by movement, but simply is eternally.

The search for knowledge of the truth reaches its zenith, when the one searching no longer identifies with all the illusory movement, apparently surrounding everything and everyone.

When the seeker stops searching around and simply watches from the perspective of the inner witness, the world turns in on itself and reveals the essential truth at the core of all.

IN REVERIE, SERENITY

Worthwhile it is, to savor the sanctuary of a few still moments, when the mind need not move or focus on anything in particular.

It is from this sacred space of serenity, that creative activity, insight and refreshed resolutions emerge.

Without the frantic pull of sensory overload and mental meandering for even a short time, nature can restore balance and reset inner compass to point once more to soul self.

As one of myriad life forms, that the One essence has taken, it is incumbent upon us to reconfigure back from whence we came.

Even the occasional experience of inner nature, like a deep tap root nourishes our whole being, giving new life to withering biological processes.

There is an obvious simplicity in stopping on occasion; to allow the great flow of life a safe passage, instead of the continual battering by waves of mind made confusion.

It is possible that if enough souls connect with their Source, a quantum shift can occur for the many, creating a more peaceful planet!

LETTING THE LIGHT IN

The trickster tries to turn inner sky gray with gloom, obscuring the bright dawn of the new days sun upon me.

The troubles this self-indulgent part of me portrays as primary are like clouds passing quickly overhead that cast dark shadows, which when viewed as the reflection of an illusion, are seen to lack substance.

Why is it so hard to wake from this wide eyed deluded dream, created by my own identification with fleeting and false delusions?

Much like the inertia of awakening from a long overdue sleep to everyday reality, the dramas set off by ego's pull to focus on darkness; makes waking up seem such an insurmountable chore.

Yet every so often, the recognition that I can be fully aware peeks through the gray layers of gunk swirling around me, allowing the bright light of awakened realization, which is my true identity, to flash through.

Simply remembering this dazzling light in times of gloomy darkness is the key to getting through illusory night, created by the great prankster ego that I have been to myself, and will eventually dispel with the light of true Self.

THE LIBERATED ONE

Latent within each precious life lives the Liberated One.

Letting clues come to the existence of such a One inside, is why so many journey on so many quests, to find answers to the ever-elusive truth or what to make of it all.

To receive replies one simply must Stop so much outer activity, look within and listen intently for the murmur of inner heart speaking.

Once heard, heart of hearts begins to enunciate from every living thing, cementing the awareness that everyone and everything is connected.

Ego will quickly step in, attempting to cover over this cosmic consciousness, with many veils of individuation, separation, doubt and fear.

To avoid suffering long under this self-inflicted illusory play, pray for the grace to find Ones who are established in their inner freedom.

Once found, they can call out that similar inner quality, which like a benevolent infection will devour ego's hold, bringing the bold, beautiful, liberated soul to full fruition once more.

MELTING MENTAL ICE

There is a thaw in the icy constriction around the heart, when the sight of sunlight alone causes a soaring of spirit.

When mind made ice starts to melt, the marvels which have always surrounded one's being begin to manifest.

Like new sprouts in the spring, renewed vision fills eyes with the wonder of infancy once again.

Mistaking mental shadows, cast from a constriction of consciousness, as reality, is the madness of the mundane, making for a cold frozen existence.

Seeing the sunlight of true being within the heart of hearts even at a glance, is enough to bring the warmth of wonder, which stirs the soul to seek the light within once more.

ON BEING IN CONTINUAL CONTENTMENT

Continual contentment with life, no matter the outcome, is the context for fulfillment.

For buried in every heart is the still small voice which must be heard!

Mental machinations and dreary distractions can drown out the whispers within.

But nothing ever totally silences that inner wellspring of wisdom, which is ever one with the universal sea of serenity.

Simply tuning in from time to time is prescription enough, for a life filled with satisfaction.

But when the sound of that voice within takes on the roar of one who is lion hearted, a steady stream of tranquility ensues.

In allowing a clear channel to that deepest core of certainty within, outcomes from actions take on transcendence, no longer holding the doer bound to further results.

The wealth of heightened well-being, with its attendant jewels of joy and fulfillment, decorate the life of one who has embraced complete communication with the One within, who speaks through the hearts of all.

ON COMPLETION

A circuit is complete only when there is connection.

So too in any endeavor of life, completion comes only after having first connected with the great cycle of consciousness, calling everything back to center.

Even in everyday functions such as eating, matter or food must be digested, in order to transform into life-force energy.

In fully assimilating what life brings into our beings, transmutation to higher frequencies of energy can occur, which can take our seemingly ordinary consciousness back to its Source.

Just like the electricity, which powers the present technological society, the energy which powers our very life-being, experienced by everyone, is never completely understood.

From where does this energy come from, and where does it go when a body ceases to function?

These questions have puzzled mystified and frustrated humanity for eons!

A few great beings have the answer, and tap on the window of our consciousness; they act as jump starters for the mystical, to connect us with what we already are, and thereby close the circuit to create completion.

ON LIVING IN *KALI YUGA

Ruminations of a ranting, restless recluse appear to rage off this page.

Regretful ramblings of a mindless press appear everywhere. If only they could refrain from sharing so much pain. And so, we too settle for the smut of the crude underbelly of what is supposed to be celebrity culture, where corrupt and crass creations are poured into our collective consciousness, and where cementing vice as virtue into impressionable minds rules.

Living in the age where the great paradox of publicity, outweighs the public good, and twists any sense of common decency into an unrecognizable mix of self-serving speculations on morality, which further fuel the fire of outrage, for the sake of ratings and monetary gain!

Given the conundrum of this time, where sex and gossip are all the rage; the sages of old have foretold of such an age, and give it the name of *Kali the destroyer. For when the deconstruction of human values is revered, the opposite can too, gather force.

As the physicist have so decreed, for every action there is an equal and opposite reaction.

And so it is said, from the same tongue comes poison or antidote, which is nectarine, never-ending bliss. Speaking words of comfort and compassion, to instill uplifment and gifts of perfect peace, pass beyond prayers to those who have ears to hear. In bygone ages eons ago, those same sages said, that great battles were fought with words, which had the power to destroy or heal.

These great mantras of old, can once again be revered, and heard reverberating within the heart's very soul, where true power resides. Simply remembering

---

*KALI YUGA-refers to the last of four ages; the present age of moral and spiritual decadence.
*Kali-refers to the Hindu goddess associated with death and destruction.

sounds of the Source, some call God, can indeed reverse the course we are on. And so in *Shiva's cosmic dance, destruction must have its stance, but what comes through is the grace to create a righteous age, whereby men will seek more to comfort and console, singing the song of universal Soul.

---

*Shiva-refers to one of the Hindu trinity of gods, representing God as the destroyer; also the name of the all pervasive supreme reality.

ON TRUE ABUNDANCE

On this overcast day, let *Lakshmi have her say, in whatever way.

Waters of life run through me, whether I let myself feel the wetness which blesses, or become a drip, and fear drowning in my own fluidity.

Fragile is the fine line, between fertility of understanding and facing fears of vulnerability.

Maybe the Goddess extends her gifts, so that perceptions can include how perishable material prosperity can be?

For to see abundance of spirit where it truly resides, means to open without reservation to the infinite reservoir of love, hidden within the human heart.

In order for this to occur, grace in all her glory, must met the receptive receptacle of a seeker's desire for fulfillment.

Then the mystical magic of Lakshmi's power, can unfold gifts which never rust or tarnish, but shine with golden brilliance as the peace which passes all understanding, within the core of every human soul.

---

*Lakshmi-refers to the Hindu Goddess of wealth and prosperity, both material and spiritual.

ONLY INFINITY

A chill comes over me, as I ponder the infinitesimal nature of my existence.

If I am made of the same stuff as the stars, then what of the earth element which remains?

Mortality of the outer shell flashes by, in the blink of an eye.

Yet soul self remains, an ever present permeating essence within everything that is!

Tried and true mental fabrications cannot hold but a drop of the infinite ocean, from which consciousness comes and soon returns to.

Like the child on the shore, trying to fit the ocean in a cup are we.

The sage's say, throw the cup to the sea and so become that which you already are!

Just, "to be or not to be," is indeed the question, as the great soliloquy says.

But the answer is neither, for to be implies we had a beginning and so have an end, when in cosmic reality, there is only infinity.

OPENING A PATH

Pathfinders of peace are those, in whom an open channel exists between heart and mind.

Soul speaks through inner songs, which are not so much heard as heartfelt, these must be translated so that understanding can emerge.

Ordinarily the mental meanderings of mind are transfixed, as the sole standard of consciousness, when indeed this is only a small part of the whole.

Given the turmoil most humans ascribe to ordinary inner reality and the world surrounding, is it any wonder that most intuit something lacking.

Yet what is most elusive, sits within the center of the human chest, like a treasure waiting for discovery.

The path leading to this elixir of life, lies still, simply waiting to be opened.

Once heart-opening beckons and recognition occurs, there is no turning back as this sublime gift allows mind to be at peace, and remember who truly inhabits the fullness of being.

THE PERFECTION OF A PRESENT MOMENT

Sitting in the shadow of my past, while looking at the rising future horizon, I can not be anywhere but here and now!

Fretting over future possibilities can only create foreboding, while dwelling on the past, presupposes the utter futility of having any effect on what has already occurred.

The freedom of simply being is to be ever present in this very moment, with a full and open awareness of all that is occurring.

When fully present, I feel able to flow with the many currents of creation coming to me.

The fluidity of being in the now and here, allows me to redirect my energetic attention around, over or through obstacles that present themselves.

Furthermore, merging with every moment makes me more potent in every action, transcending limitations of time, space and expectations.

Even though making the present tense primary is as natural as breathing, still the illusions of past and future can haunt the moment if allowed.

Perfection is not in some seventh heaven, nor in the blissful nothingness of amnesic sleep, but simply the gift I give myself as a present moment.

REFLECTING ON ME

Nostalgia for what once was grips me now, even though I'm still living through its reverberating ripples.

The déjà vu of being the child again through adult eyes causes my inner being to cry for what once was and perhaps still is.

If I could met the young boy who was me, I would probably say all the things he could be, knowing full well that destiny's decree, can be swayed by degrees to an ever new way.

So what of this feeling of being the kid of my past, as I see life once again unfolding it's never ending repast of possibilities, through the eyes of my son?

The rising future beckons continuity of sorts; still a new perspective arises with sharing what was and is now, with a generation to come.

In fully living my life, I can but insure that the young eyes that watch will concur, that it is good to be immersed in the stuff of life, but to also create a space for the serenity of solitude, to take hold in it's midst.

For to truly live well and full, one must fulfill in every way the decree, to be true to oneself and thus, to all others too.

REMEMBERING ONENESS

Perceiving two or more makes mortality a chore, instead of marveling at *Maya's* great opera called life.

Where only oneness is remembered, there is the ecstasy of elevated understanding, which can uplift our spirit back to Source.

Settling for a vision of separation, is dancing with duality, without knowing who wrote the score or choreographed the show.

How is it that we feel we are not greater than the sum of the whole, when indeed we are that and more?

There can only be a shadow because light is obstructed; similarly in the realm of so called everyday reality, are we not identifying with our shadows, instead of the light Source which creates them.

To truly enjoy the dramas we create is it not better to remember who plays the role, rather than believing we are the part we play.

For when the actor forgets his true identify and believes he is the part he plays, is he not ready for the asylum.

It is much better to never forget, that being one with whatever comes is much more fun!

Maya's-refer to page 60.

RIPPLES OF CONSCIOUSNESS

Ripples are we, ever receding into the great sea of consciousness.

Taking form as a wave that continues into infinitude, appearing to move but staying ever the same in essence.

The energy, which is one with Source, sings on in us always.

Just as a mirage appears shimmering on the horizon of a great desert, beckoning weary travelers with the promise of shade and refreshment; so too, do the many forms and objects take shape within mind's eye, leading the one infinite consciousness to believe it can take refuge within these illusions, when really it is only a reflection of itself!

So what can be taken from the perfect or added?

Instead, allow the perception of perfection, to concur with what we really are.

As ripples and waves recede into a shore once more, they never really end.

Water becomes one with earth, air and ether, only to continue on reforming, remerging and reconnecting to the one consciousness again and again.

SEEING OUR SOURCE

Fresh outlooks are needed, in order to renew perspective with ourselves and the world surrounding.

Few forms of preconceptions prevail, in one who sees with eyes prepared to view what is.

As the prescription of our glasses change, things can come into focus or become more obscured.

When the true seer is allowed to shine through, vision becomes clearer and all encompassing.

The world becomes as we see it!

Recognition comes, that the shadow is not to be feared, when the object represented is finally seen in the light of expanded awareness.

Truly, until consciousness perceives it's own brilliant bursting luminescence, everything and everyone appears as a poor reflection; never satisfying the primal urge to merge with what is the Source of all.

SEEING WITH THE WHOLE OF BEING

Refracted light reflected resembles what is, but a mirage is whatever it seems to be.

The image that a retina takes in comes together in the back of the brain to form something that can be identified as a sight.

Why believe our eyes, when a pinpoint of bright light in the night sky is just now arriving after a million years of travel?

Believing is more of seeing than any sight can convey!

For all that is seen must first be translated through the filter of mind's eye.

Settling for superficial seeing, is the same as a thirsty traveler lost in a desert, drinking the sand of a mirage oasis.

True vision comes, when illusory seeing is done; only then can awakening dawn to the view of the one inner eye, which when opened sees with the whole of being.

SEEKING THE SOURCE OF LIFE

So many discordant voices saying so many different things, yet speaking from the same place within.

Seemingly separate souls searching for the great similarity, which unites us in our seeking the elusive elixir of life.

What is this gnawing knowledge, which most conscious beings intuit is there as a forgotten thought, just on the tip of the tongue.

Some say it is only to be found in the heaven of our afterlife, or in the nirvana of blissful deep meditations.

Yet some sages say, look not outside for the answer to this conundrum, but simply change perspective and view life with the awareness which awaits notice.

For it is consciousness itself which we seek, which is the same Source of all seeking.

A burst of energy emanates from the one thought to be; are we not the continuation of this emanation, and at the same time its origin!

SEEKING EUPHORIA

What is this Elusive Euphoria we all seek?

Comes through consciousness for a peek, gone in a flash, just as fast.

One moment in ecstasy, the next back to doldrums.

From hum drum to ecstatic and back, racing headlong into the abyss, we miss only that from which it all comes.

Who can be so quick as to hold onto quicksilver?

Or mistake the shadow, from that which it's cast.

The poet in his epiphany knows, that senses can only perceive so far.

The benevolent brilliance shinning through sensations, always returns to the center of joy; just remember heart core, and we are there once more.

SOARING INSTEAD OF WHORING

Soaring on currents of contentment is as simple as opening oneself to the winds of change, so that they blow through and uplift, instead of blow away.

Tendencies to cling with gravity, by curling into a defensive ball of contracted crud, are overcome by allowing rather than resisting what comes.

As a bird opens it's wings, the wind effortlessly takes this magnificent creature to flight; in a similar way, as a human opens their heart, compassion naturally suffuses through them into all they make contact with, uplifting not only their own spirit, but countless others they meet on their way.

Then instead of whoring through life, selling soul for approval and outer well-being, the human spirit can soar free, flying over obstacles by simply allowing the thermal winds of divinity to float them lightly through life.

SWAYING IN ONE'S OWN BLISSFUL BREEZE

The trees sway, as if in appreciation of the breeze.

Similarly the body moves with life, solely as a consequence of the breath, that constantly flows through it.

From where do these movements come from, whether breath, breeze or cosmic wind?

The origin of all is but the simple subtle wish to be, which expanded out from the ever blissful being-ness of Source.

With this wishful will, washing over all of existence as the tidal wave, some say was the big bang, we are all wet With the vibration emanating*OM, out into infinity.

Whether baby's cry of joy or dying death rattle, all is in continual movement, set in motion by a perfect wish.

It is only when ego's will believes itself greater than this force that the friction created, causes anguish and pain.

Once balance is restored, in recognition of the perfection of our Source, we can again sway in the blissful breeze of our own connection to all.

---

* *OM*-refers to the primordial sound or vibration from which the universe sprang.

THE INVISIBLE FORCE

Ripples on still waters, rustling leaves in the trees, all telltale signs of the invisible force which moves through all things.

What of this corporeal body, which is thought to be alive?

What animates the senses and flows through the breath?

Perhaps this unseen power, which holds planets in their orbits, allows consciousness of itself to manifest in the minds of men.

Maybe within the spaces between all apparent objects is the essence of all creation, flowing on infinitely, infusing everything with itself.

So in the seed of the atom is the original Adam, prototype replicating itself, but when the apple of limited knowledge was bitten, the atom split and the destructive power of ego's duality, was unleashed onto the field of awareness.

Inherent in the cosmology of man is the essential freedom of will to choose the limitation and separation of ego's dual vision, leading to (M.A.D.), Mutually Assured Destruction; or returning to the Oneness of the invisible force, which is always tranquil and at peace with itself.

THE JOY OF CREATION

Creating something when there was nothing is such a rush; it allows an opportunity to be again in alignment with true Source, from where we have all come.

Moments of elation occur, in that timeless space from which the creative process emerges.

In those moments, individuality of ego submerge and the identity we are born to live shines forth, as a bright new day in our universal life.

From the perspective of Creativity, there is only what is happening in this moment which is primary, everything else of past and future fade to the background noise of mediocrity.

All the great ones who have walked this way whether inventors, great thinkers or artists have embodied the fusion of spontaneity, ability and the simple joy of making something, which has never been thought possible, a reality manifest.

In that moment, when the wish to be one with what is occurring transpires, we are transported to the realm of unity with Creator, and so transfixed in the experience of creation, are infused with the bliss of it all.

THE SKY'S THE LIMIT AND THEN SOME

Welcome back Blue sky's my soul cries, as clouds finally clear, after what felt like an almost eternal gloom.

Bringing back a clear day from dark foreboding overcast grayness, is like shifting from the black and white Kansas, to Oz filled with brilliant colors.

Beautiful blue azure, seemingly limitless and vast, patched here and there with puffs of white moisture; where is it that this life-sustaining envelope we call atmosphere, touches infinite space?

In reflecting on such awe-inspiring beauty, I must ponder where indeed must my individuality, which gives ego personality life, meet the universality of infinity.

Perhaps only in these wonders that stagger comprehension, can the mind stop long enough to experience in stillness, the true Source of outer and inner sky, which is limitless, and in this knowledge partake of the oneness of it all.

THE WAY OF LIGHT

Curse the darkness, or find a light.

Choice is always inherent, in the apparent dilemma, of seeking solutions in the maze of modern life.

Finding those who can take us from darkness, which is the ignorance of our true nature, to the light of self-knowledge, which is the true luminescence of life, is key to the way of light!

Wisdom is a word worth pondering, but as of late, being considered wise has come into some misuse, implying cunning and dishonesty, sometimes in the vernacular.

Where before, the same word meant one who lived through the hard-earned school of experience and applied philosophical truths to everyday reality.

This indeed is living by the light, becoming a beacon for others in ordinary ways.

Any illumination or guidance can only come, from one who has been willing to walk through obstacles and conquer their own dark nights of soul.

Seeking knowledge through the luminous way, first find one who has mastered their own path to the inner light which illumines all, then follow these beacons of wisdom into the bright bliss of luminosity.

THE TREASURED GIFTS OF AWARENESS

Gifts and blessings pour down at every moment on everyone, but unless the many layers covering receptivity are removed, their effects go unnoticed.

Like a thick malaise, the layers of illusory mental menageries obscure the wonders occurring in every moment.

What inspires awe, in one whose senses are clear to perceive the great abundant treasure which is this life, are taken for just ordinary everyday reality, by the majority of others, whose minds are coated with a soothe, appearing as mediocrity.

Like newly fallen snow flakes', whose crystalline structure is at once beautiful and totally unique in every way, our moments come, forming a splendid mosaic of existence, which is a marvel in its individuality and majestic in its union with all.

So seek the clarity of awareness to conceive, that in this very instant, the summation of all creation is at once within our perception, surrounding all that can be perceived.

If indeed this treasured vision is hidden within, then all that is needed is focused awareness of that which surrounds and enfolds us, to uncover our true wealth, of the precious moment.

THE TRUTH OF WHAT IS SOUGHT

Blue skies of a clear not obscured life, make clarity no longer a concern.

When vision is clouded over by worries, fears and other false facades, the freedom to truly perceive what is can be impaired.

So to search for clear vistas of our truth, is often about rising above the cloudy dark layers of our own making.

The sky is always blue, so why should we not be able to cut through our deluded states of wrong understanding, to the knowledge of what is true?

When awareness of our truth calls us back, to becoming established in whom we really are, no further seeking is necessary, as the realization comes, we are That which we seek!

ACKNOWLEDGEMENTS

First and foremost, I'm very happy to thank my wonderful wife Mary Jane for her love, support and assistance with formatting and editing this work.

I'm especially grateful to John Calabrese, Editor-At-Large of Creations Magazine and Transpersonal Psychotherapist, without whose encouragement, this book may never have become a reality. John's intrepid support throughout this project and his great editing have been invaluable.

Particular thanks are owed to Lorena Rostig, for her many inspired creative suggestions and for her brilliant project management, which made this book possible. My great appreciation goes out to Annelise Rostig, for her gifted vision of capturing in photographs, the images in this work.

To my dear friend and fellow poet Elliott Berman, who through his life and death was an inspiration to me and countless others.

To all those many innumerable, loving and gifted presences within my life—of parents, illumined teachers, mentors, colleagues, clients, Siddha Yoga students who are incarcerated, family and friends—whose influence and support made it possible for me to write the many inspired words contained within these pages.

Finally, to my two great children Linda and Jeff, who never tire of hearing their dad's poetry.

Get Published, Inc!
Thorofare, NJ 08086
08 September 2009
BA2009251